My second book... Wow. I want to first thank God for the talent to write, to express myself when speaking just doesn't cut it. Thank you to my readers for your support. Words cannot express how humbled I am to have your support. It is my hope that reading this book of poems, you see my growth from my first book, Pieces of Me, (available on Amazon and yes shameless plug). This book of poems simply examines the different journeys we must take and the lessons in those journeys. It will not always be a happy ending, but it will always be a learned experienced. Enjoy.

TABLE OF CONTENTS

Journey through this compilation of poems that ignite the heart through the lens of a poet's experiences of love, loss, heartbreak, and hope.

Love Yourself

Society will have you thinking,
Surgically modified bod es is where it's at.
The more your waist is shrinking
The appeal is on a booty that's round and fat.
Don't stop there, go and get lip injections
Dye your hair some unnaturally blonde color
Every man loves this look, there's no exception
Superficial beauty is the only allure.
Who you are on the inside doesn't matter,
You're only meant to be on display.
Even with all the men you flatter
You see more change should be underway.
The more you alter you outside appearance
The more you hurt on the inside.
The person you were, she's long gone, in disappearance
The pain within doesn't subside.
You want to be loved for what lies internal
You have more to offer you swear.
But they refuse to look past what's external
You're like furniture, an overly decorated chair.
Can all the work you've had done be reversed?
As you attempt to get you back.
What you once saw as a blessing you now feel you're cursed
A small waist, fat butt, fried and dyed hair was never where it's at.

Thy Shall Know Your Worth

Too often we allow men to occupy a place in our hearts when all he really wants is a moment in our bed.

Too often we give men husband privileges expecting him to fall in line when at the end of the day all he really wants is sex.

We allow him to stroke us into submission and thrust us into oblivion only to be left abandoned in the morning.

Tell me queen when was the last time you rejoiced over a good man instead of grieve in mourning over a bad one?

See he's not bad because he took advantage of what you put out.

He's not bad because he loved you down in the sheets just to put you out.

He's bad because that's the side you let him see of you.

Rather than sit and talk, you were in a rush to get in his room.

Stop selling yourself to someone who isn't even worth your bid.

Stop giving your heart to someone dressed as a man, but in reality he's still a kid.

I know you saw the different game systems in every room

What makes you think you ain't a conquest too?

Boys play the chasing game, and run towards the next once they've put a stake in their claim.

Then will convince you you're crazy, just so you'll feel ashamed as they mind fuck you again and again.

Take your place my queens and refuse to step in his home without even knowing his story.

Stop allowing him to deposit his demons in your treasure, only to repeat history.

Love yourself more than the idea of a body lying next to you

Because when he awakes, he just sees a corpse in you.

He bodied that body you thought he would caress with promises of a future.

It's time to push fantasies aside and see the reality of the situation.
Life isn't a fairy tale wait ng to happen to you just because you
behave as a damsel in distress.
You ought to focus on yourself and allow God to do the rest.
He will bring you the man that will take his time to understand all of
you and the hidden crevices of your mind.
The kind of man who will touch you with his words not just his dick in
record time.
Stop being like a microwave, quickly heated up just for a thirty
second fuck
Then have the audacity to wonder why men are all amuck
When it's you that's got your worth fucked up.
Cherish yourself to understand not every joker should have access
to your promise land.
Carry your self-esteem high and allow God to bring you your guy
A man who will appreciate your outward beauty but always first take
care what's inside.

To THOT or not to THOT

(THOT is an acronym that stands for that hoe over there)

So for all you females screaming niggas ain't shit
Because they don't show appreciation
Talking about all they wanna do is hit
Then your value decreases in depreciation
It's not all his fault.
You walk around barely dressed showing off your hips and legs
Thinking he won't have naughty thoughts
How's he supposed to know you smart in the head
When you advertising your body like you waiting to be caught.
Nah he ain't thinking about what you bring to the table or if you could
be a wife
He worried about what lies in between them thighs and how many
turns he can get in one night.
You idolize watching Amber Rose
Be exposed and think of her as hero.
Don't you notice and see
After sexing her body
Being with her was a no.
Don't look to Kim K thinking she's the way
When her relevance lies in the curves of her hips
And what she did with them lips
You're much more than that.
It's not shade, no hate, honestly I'm just trying to educate
Just because you get attention all due to a tiny waist
It won't win you first place anywhere unless it's at his place.
Be aware it's just a thrill and once he's gotten his fill,
He wants you gone and might even throw a few bills.
So now you're deduced to something like a prostitute,

The next man is waiting to put you to use.
So my sisters and counterparts, lead with your mind instead of your body parts.
Let him see you for you outside of what you can do,
Cause once that's established he's through.

Brown Girl

Once upon time my color was seen as a crime so they made us question our design by attacking our minds and desecrating our spines.
It wasn't hard to do since we already felt beneath you, so we allowed the pain you put us through in constant fear we had no one to turn to.
How were we to accept our color wasn't an abomination, a result of decades of segregation for we were perceived as the intimidation.
Had we known our strength and just how flexible we could be when bent, imagine the years free our ancestors could have spent.
See when you perceive one as a threat you capitalize on their being inept so they are in debt to you and after you, they have no one left.
We were ripped from our families and forced to raise their families so sadly our offspring didn't know us as family.
Even now we are supposed free, we are still in captivity suffering from anxiety and insecurity all because I am not as light as she.
Forgive me in that the sun loved my skin a direct result of all this melanin and I no longer see myself as sin.
Different shades of black I am blessed with, indicative of my strength, my perseverance, my resilience, yet I am still seen as unfit.
For I bear the scars of the many, who were shamed because they look like me and thought they were a monstrosity because they were shunned by society.
Shaping their beliefs from birth, they couldn't see their worth, how

9

much more pain could they endure, the elasticity expired, they lost their girth.

I refuse to give you power over me Massa no matter how much society allows you to attack us

I will overcome.

You knew our worth back then and you see our worth now, I will not bow down like them, I will rise and make them proud.

Their struggles weren't in vain for me to keep singing the same tune that life ain't fair for a negro.

Why don't you watch from your pedestal how this negro is determined to grow despite your disdain and ego, I am my own hero.

Distortion

The woman who stares back at me
Is tired and worn out.
She is visibly unhappy
Desperately seeking a way out.
The misery is too much to bare
Her scars have scars
All this time she's been unaware
Of the growing damage on her heart.
He's the only man she's ever known
Without him she'd be lost,
With him, she's established a home
Of immeasurable cost.
Eyes that once held much promise
Now are sunken in, close to death.
She finds herself joyless
She experiences loss of breath.
Migraines come quite often
There seems to be no peace,
If she stays, her fate is in a coffin
Still, she can't find strength to leave.
She is chained to him
Her heart carries his name.
Despite their future being grim
She fears she'll never love this way again.
As she stares at her reflection
All the hurt etched on her once blemish free face
She convinces herself she's the exception

And by his side is her place.

Outer Body

I watch myself transform around you into this angry woman
Who behaves as if you're her enemy.
Her body language suggests hatred toward you
And she doesn't know why.
After many years of being together and fighting for your love
She's not sure if it was worth it.
The sacrifices.
The energy.
The love she once felt.
All gone as if they never existed.
Who she is to you now is a broken woman.
She's got nothing to offer other than the offspring that keeps you
there.
Practiced smiles.
Forced attraction.
She feels trapped.
In all the murkiness, she wants to find peace.
In all the tension, she wants to experience joy.
She wants to feel the love she once felt for you
Instead of the indifference that plagues her.
She wants to long for your touch again
Instead of shrug away when your arms come reach out to embrace
her.
So I tell her, "let it go and it will come"
She's confused by "it"
For "it" keeps her angry.
Stuck in a frenzied space that only breeds contempt.

Transfixed by the wrongdoings against her which she hasn't forgiven.
Enamored with being right not realizing being right leaves you alone.
"Let it go" I say once more.
"The anger. The hurt. The disappointment. The hate. The sorrow.
The silence."
She looks to me, desperation in her eyes wanting to do just that.
She shakes her head adamantly knowing it's not possible
She's no longer listening as she turns the key to the door only to
become angry woman again.

Duality

The two sides of me
Are in constant conflict.
The side that behaves sensibly
And knows you aren't who I should be with.
She refuses to get sucked into your lies
She will not accept your apologies.
She knows being with you is a waste of time
And the importance of reciprocity.
She doesn't take your call
After yet another broken word.
She's done giving you her all
After spending so much time being unheard.
She doesn't cry for you
She is much too strong for that
She won't be your fool
Don't think she'll look back.

She desires to be brave and leave, but then there's the other side.

The one that's weak for you
Set on being your ride or die.
The one who'll bleed for you
If it means saving your life.
She'll give you chance after chance
No matter the amount of hurt you cause
She'll trust one day you'll grow up and be a man

Maturity will eventually shed your flaws.
She'll justify your wrongs
And accept your empty excuses
Just so you two can get along
She'll endure different abuses.
She will hold on tighter
Despite the many times you break away.
She reasons she's just a fighter
And it's weaker to leave than to stay.

The combination of such calamity within me keeps me bound by your side.

Hurt People Hurt

Just me and my thoughts
A volatile place to be.
Mind and heart are distraught
It's her against me.
My mind wants one thing
While my heart pleads the other way.
Thinking of the joy you used to bring
A simple gesture made my day.
I have to let you go
You have no place here.
With you I couldn't grow
All that existed was fear.
Pondering when you would leave
Because one day you'd want more.
The love you beg to receive
Would leave you feeling insecure.
You're worth more than I can give
My value decreases over time.
Despite your being the reason I live
I refuse to take away your shine.
You need someone strong
Who knows herself intricately;
Knows where she belongs
Doesn't buy into the opinions of society.
I watch you give your all to me

As I struggle to give you half.
All that's left are fragments of me
I'm still broken from the past.
I don't understand what you see within
When all I feel is less than,
Under all this made up skin
Is a fragile, scared woman.
I thought I could fake it with you
Along the way, my walls would eventually crumble
Even with the way you've always pursued
My heart, I continue to fumble.
I can't be a complete part of you,
When inside I'm still recovering
It doesn't matter what you do,
I still hold on to my suffering.

The selfish part of me,
Can't seem to let you go
She wants to love you completely,
You're what feeds her soul.
She desires to let you in
She knows you are a healing,
She's unsure where to begin,
She leans upon her feelings.
Trusting you won't run,
Instead you'll be a point of rescue.
You'll be the only one
Who's privy to all she's been through.
You'll hold her the nights she screams,
From the past terrors she's endured.

Reassure her that you're a team,
In you, she can feel secured.
Despite her attempts to give you an exit,
You won't give in to her sabotage.
You question when she will get it
Your love for her isn't a mirage.
Because she refuses to accept,
Your love as unconditional and true,

How could you have possibly been prepped,
When she reveals she's been sleeping around on you?

7 Minutes

Let me have seven minutes of your time
To explain my transgressions.
I know hurting you was a major crime
When all you deserved was my protection.
I'll admit to you I wasn't ready
For any serious commitment.
But I couldn't see you without me
You were that angel, heaven sent.
Maybe I was selfish for being with them
When you should've been suffice.
I promise they all were just friends
Women who I slept with from time to time.
Just wait a minute I still have a few minutes left,
To tell you how much you mean to me.
You're still the one that takes away my breath
And accepting you gone just ain't easy.
So let me take this last minute
To make this plea.
My life ain't shit without you in it
I know you agree.
I didn't mess up because I didn't see your worth
Truth is I always knew you were rare,
I didn't understand how to put you first
Because I assumed you'd always stay there.
I miss your carefree smile and effortless beauty
The way you squint your eyes, when trying to understand me.

I miss the love I don't deserve
And the way you fit perfectly beside me.
I long to feel up on your curves
To once again be the man to envy.
I threw it all away,
Just to maintain a certain image
I promise I'm a different man today
Internally there's no longer a scrimmage.
Seven minute encounters with women I saw no future with
All along you were what I needed.
There's not a thing I could do to change it
Except admit I should've heeded.
Don't walk away from me I beg of you
You're the one I need to be with
I will do whatever it takes to show you,
Just give me seven more minutes.

Homonyms

He has his eyes set on her, she's his next prey
He feeds on the fact she's insecure, someone please pray.
He's not interested in what she's got to give, he just wants a piece
He only knows he finds her attractive and wants to disrupt her peace.
She gives him a chase, oh how it turns him on when she says no
He can see the longing on her face, too bad she doesn't know.
She's just another notch on his belt, he only thinks of what will be won
Once he's done pleasing himself, she'll be left like the other ones.
He doesn't even stop to consider the hurt that she'll go through
The time she'll spend being bitter, focused on the constant compliments he threw.
She won't trust another soul, she'll only look out for "I"
She'll wander around aimlessly, an empty hole and tear stained eyes.
He'll easily move along not a second thought of how she's been affected
She'll choose a lifetime of being alone, she vows to never again be effected.
She will always feel the void and cry late at night when no one can hear
Attempt to block out their times enjoyed, for love has no place here.

Mourning

There is power in the name of Jesus, There is power in the name of
Jesus
I could've died on the spot when mom told me you were on a hospital
bed
A piece of me shatters when she relays doctors say you're brain
dead.
How do I accept that you're leaving me when I've still got room to
grow
Dad who will I turn to if you decide to let go?
All my life, there you were, a few steps behind,
Always encouraging us all, preaching to never be afraid of our shine.
The many days you let me play horsey on your back
Despite your long day at work.
You even overcame several heart attacks
You are superman, we know your worth.
Seeing you lay lifeless on that bed breaks me in two
One side wishing you peace, the other begging you to get through.

I turn to God, raw pain emerges from my throat
Begging Him to spare you, doesn't He take account of my vote?

Perform the miracle of allowing you to open your eyes
To detach from the IV's sticking you inside.
To hear your soulful laugh that dominates the room
To one day see me at the end of the altar saying, "I do"

22

Who's going to finish showing me what it means to provide?
Who's going to build me up when I feel low inside?
You see I need you now more than ever
I won't take for granted the time we spend together.
Dad, just come back we need you here in this life
What will mom do, all she's ever known is being mother and wife.
I watch her sit in the corner struggling to take a breath
She knows what I know; this room reeks of death.
I squeeze your hand hoping you do the same.
Open your eyes, and say our names.
The constant beep from the monitor that is keeping you alive
Acts as a timer telling us how much longer you will survive.
Tears invade and flood my eyes when you don't squeeze back
The fear I feel inside is all too much when I realize this time you
won't be back.
As the monitor flatlines, mom tugs at me to let your hand go
Right in the hospital room, a piece of me is gone, I feel so low.
Powerless, I watch doctors try to resuscitate and get a pulse
I scream out loud to them to save you, it's my only impulse.
When the doctor gives the time of death, I know it's too late.
My superman is gone, I can't help but feel irate.
Despondent, in a daze I hear a voice whisper,
There is power in the name of Jesus, There is power in the name of
Jesus

Prisoner

The instant I laid eyes on you
I knew I was in a world of trouble
Naturally gravitated toward you
I didn't even know your name.
But somehow I knew your story
And knew it couldn't be complete without me
So like a rose to its stem
We were together.
Your protection held me up
And I was the pretty thing to look at.
And no matter how much admiration came from others
It was you I remained a part of.
I clutched onto you like a newborn to its mother
Inhaling your scent
Basking in your warmth
Certain of your love.
You guarded me with your life
Never allowing access to others
You created a world of our own.
Each kiss intense as if we'd never lay eyes on each other again.
Each lingering hug because we just couldn't get enough.
Simple caresses that left us both yearning for more.
Now that you're gone, it's the memories that keep me sane.
To know a love so pure, so real, I know I won't ever be the same.
I still feel your spirit alongside me as if you never left.
I still catch glimpses of you every time I take a breath.

Loving you is what nourishes my soul
Loving you is what made me whole.
I won't lay to rest the memories we shared
I'll continue to grasp on to them until I meet you over there.
Rest in eternal peace my stem, I feel you watching from above
Forever I will remain your prisoner of love.

Boy bye

I won't say that I'm over you
That just isn't true
Now that the hole is no longer in the shape of you
That's when you want to come through.
Bringing me old items that I left behind
Finding ways to express you wish you were still mine.
I want to be strong and not catapulted back
Yes you and I had a thing but you're no good for me, that's a fact.
You weren't interested in what I brought to the table
You were focused on the sex not the relationship label.
You threw me out when you learned of my intention not to yield
Being around you now feel I'm in need of a shield;
To protect my heart from someone so malevolent
It's funny you were the same person swearing you were different.
So as you stand on my doorstep looking oh so good
I'm going to ignore my heart and do what a smart woman would.
No I don't miss the times we had for they weren't genuine on your part.
No I don't want to go out and cause more damage to my heart.
There's no second chance for I am not the son of God
You should've known what you had in me instead of allowing others the job.
I'm glad you had time to think and regret what you have done
Go on and tell someone else your woes because I'm not the one.

War

They want you to choose
Between your blood and wife
I can't tell you what to do
Even if I believe it's right.
You see I understand the bond
From father to son and mother to child
Despite the fact I'm the one
They won't allow me to cramp their style.
I know they raised you with all the essentials
That much is true,
But I'm the one who sees and can help you reach your potential
In all that you dream to do.
They will make you feel guilty
Tell you be careful of the bridges you burn
Complain, that's their specialty
The result is your back being turned
On me, and that's ok
For you know I hate to see you stressed
Putting you in between a rock and hard place
Will only incite further mess.
They want to be in control
It's the only way they operate,
Anytime you tell them no
That's when they infiltrate.
I stand by alone on the sideline
Rooting for you to stand your ground

No ability to score points if you're willingly blind
Understand their goal is for me to be left without sound..
So I let them believe they've won the battle
As I suit up for war
Let them continue to prattle
They'll soon receive what they've been looking for.

Contact

I walk toward you certainty in my step
It's my intention to give you a memory you won't forget.
I stare straight into your eyes, the window to your soul
It ain't just about fucking, tonight I'll make you whole.
Before I even undress you, I'll whisper the sweet things I know you
long to hear
And just as I begin to caress you, I'll make sure to kiss you
everywhere.
In no time soon, you'll be begging me to penetrate you
I take my time, there's no need to rush, I intend to enjoy the view
Watching you strip away every article of clothing turns me to the
point of no return
Anticipation courses through my veins, no room for other concerns
When I taste you I am hooked, needing another hit,
There's no question in mind, I'm immediately an addict.
A hunger takes over me as I yearn to be inside you
I tame the beast within still taking my time with you.
I can feel the heat emanating from in between your legs beckoning
for me
So I plunge deep within you and get lost in your screams
From the way you grip my back and wrap your legs around my waist
To the way you bite my lips and look me in my face,
This moment is what we both need and desire
Contented sighs escape us both as I have just extinguished your fire.

Love Session

The way my body responds to yours is automatic
The sensation under your touch is climatic.
Reducing me to moans of pleasure
Each time you stroke and pump in my treasure.
How effortlessly you lay the pipe
By getting me just right
Ripples of orgasm after orgasm erupts within
Causes me to bite on your glistening skin.
I scratch and claw unable to control
This hold you have over my body and soul
The raspiness from my voice weak from screams
The way my body twitches as my treasure creams.
Your relentless persistence leaves me at a loss of words
Anything that was wrong is instantly cured.
I lie on you after our intense love session
Completely enthralled with all my blessings.

Do Me

Rub your head against my entrance
Tease me with a slow dance,
Move in circular motion
Stare in my eyes, I want to see emotion.
Grab my wrists and hold them tight
Kiss me as if it depends on your life.
Suck on my neck, go on and leave passion marks
Whisper in my ear the wild ride we're about to embark.
Squeeze my breasts and suck at the same time
Make me feel so good, I lose all track of time.
Move further down and kiss my wet lips,
Blow into my opening as I sensually roll my hips.
Flick your tongue over my most sensitive spot
Without warning plunge me with your manhood, instantly make me more hot.
Bring attention back to my nipples for they miss the warmth of your mouth
Keep up the momentum, make me scream, I want to shout.
Just when I'm nearing the edge of explosion
Stop abruptly and keep my legs wide open.
Pressing your member against my skin
I lead you to put it back in.
We move with urgency, the fire too intense to turn back now
The chemistry is much too palpable than the average person allows.
Our goal is the same, that is to make one another come
Two more deep, slow thrusts inside me and we both are done.

Foreplay

Eyes that bore right through me
Your nose so perfectly made
Lips begging to be kissed
A neck so decadent
I will settle my eyes on your collarbone.
Let me explore your body in ways no one else has.
Just a touch on my shoulder
Sends a shiver down my spine
The heat will not be smoldered
I yearn to make you mine
Breasts so supple
Nipples erect
I can tell you're ready
But.
 I'm not finished yet.
Allow me to admire the creation before me.
I study each finger adorned onto you
Mindlessly entangling mine with yours.
Stroking ever so gently, like a woman in mourning.
Let me comfort you as we lay to rest the men of your past.
And celebrate the life we are bound to create.
Your breathing while even, becomes a tad staggered.
I can tell you're anxious,
As I unwrap my hands from yours
My fingers do a dance down your abdomen.
Just like silk, my fingers slip into your fire.

You gasp. I gasp. Both filled with desire.
The more you move on my fingers, the less control I have.
To gain composure, I must pull my fingers back.
The crazed look in your eyes, I push aside
As I explore your branches:
Beautifully sculpted legs, supporting an Amazon.
Dainty toes, I dare to enclose with my mouth.
Licking away at your troubles, sucking the pain from running after
men who didn't treat you right.
You squirm and giggles emerge
I know you're on the verge
Of losing it.
My eyes are similar to an addict; shifty not sure where to remain.
As you lay there begging for it,
I am frozen in awe, your body embedded in my membrane.
One last look in your eyes,
I am sure of what to do next, I imagine your surprise
When I say to you, "Get dressed, some other time we'll have sex"

Chambers

I long to be the the parts of your heart that sustain you
For my love to course through your veins and pump like atriums do.
Let my love be the oxygen that is needed to keep you feeling invincible.
My actions will behave something like the right ventricle;
Receive my love as the oxygenated blood coming from your lungs
Don't focus on the what was, in this moment I'm your only one.
If you let me, my undying love will pump into the rest of your body
Like the left ventricle, the strongest chamber, nothing will ever stop me.
I'll be the excitement you crave after a long stressful day at work
I'll be the relaxation you need, a refuge from the hurt.
Pumping endlessly to give you the love you deserve
Your happiness will always come first.
I will continuously work on different ways to fulfill you
Like arteries, my love will travel throughout your body to consume you
I will pay especially close attention to your intricate parts
Similar to capillaries, only good things will I impart.
No there's not a need to worry if I will slack
Just like veins, my love will always give back.
Understanding and wholly acknowledging the function of your heart
Let me remain your center, I vow we never will part.

Corporate

They reel you in with the "we want diversity" spiel
Only to find out that they weren't being real.
They want us uniform, in speaking and how we dress
Don't you dare voice your opinion because that's when you get stressed.
All of a sudden you're not a team player, you stick out like a sore thumb
You start to get write ups and verbal warnings, one more mistake and you're done.
What happened to freedom of speech and your rights as an individual?
You start to seek a way out entertaining the idea of income that's residual.
That too is a scam and you're too bright to fall for that
But the loans are mounting up, you feel the burden on your back.
How do you survive in a world of followers when you're meant to be a leader?
You invest in yourself and take risks soon you'll attract other believers.
Refuse to sell yourself short, working day after day for someone else
Get off that slave ship and hustle harder than anyone else.
You are sure to break into a realm that only houses success
Then you can give corporate your ass to kiss, because you are now among the best.

Edge

The more I tried to ignore you
The more difficult it became
To be myself.
The more I allowed you to mistreat me
The more I felt I was being drained.
Using so much energy to contain myself
As if I were the issue.
Using self constraint to not say anything
After the constant abuse
This ends today.
I will say what I need to say.
Like bile threatening to erupt
I could no longer swallow my hurt.
You wanted to see me mess up
Just to see me fired from work.
I unleashed my pain.
I unleashed my misery.
Hoping to free myself from this chain
Of endless negativity.
I could've laid my hands on you
As you smirked at my eruption
But after all I've been through
I won't give into more corruption.
How disappointed I became in myself
To allow someone of such little significance
To take me out of my element.
In refusing to stomach your assaults on me

Over the brink I went.

No I'm not sorry, so I won't apologize
You've got to understand and realize
The breaking point I reached.
To free myself, I needed to speak.
So fuck you and the seniority you think you have.
I have someone much more powerful who has my back.
As you take pride in what you elicited from me
Just know this job is your final destination
I've got better things in store for me.

Mister Wrong

They try to convince me that I was the victim
They try to soothe me with words of encouragement.
Truth is I just wish I could get you out my system
Get you off my mind and forget the times we spent.
You were my first love, the man I placed on a pedestal
You taught me much about myself, especially things I didn't want to
see
For the way you played me, your performance deserves a medal
The countless times you preached jealousy didn't suit me.
My heart still pounds furiously in my chest
At the sound and thought of your name.
I can hardly accept memories are only what's left
And how I constantly take the blame.
Why wasn't I good enough for you?
What about me didn't fit?
Was there anything in my power I could do?
To show you without me you couldn't be shit.
Time is showing me how well you are living
And how easily you have abandoned me.
One would think no cares would be given
But I still love you with all of me.
It's like the moment you came into my life
Your presence continued to ricochet,
I won't lie, I certainly believed I would be your wife
Share that home and white picket fence with you one day.
Day after day it's a constant reminder that you've clearly moved on

I'll find the strength to do the same and accept that you were just my Mr. Wrong.

Secret

I've remained tight lipped about a certain transgression
One night I was in someone else's possession.
The same tongue that I caress you with tasted his body.
My hands intertwined in his as if he belonged to me.
Passion marks left behind
Standing out, screeching out our crime.
I lay in his arms, stretched out against him
The electricity palpable, skin against skin.
In that one night I destroyed everything that I mean to you
I sadly wear my "A,", I am no longer a woman of virtue.
I don't deserve your forgiveness for I behaved like cowards do.
Running to find solace in another instead of sharing my qualms with you.
I cannot find it in me to confess my breach of trust
I refuse to jeopardize a future that doesn't include us.
So I keep my secret caged within, the lie burns in my chest.
I know not telling you is the option that's best.
I'll endure my demons, constantly tormenting me
Invading my thoughts, calling me out on my adultery.
I'll plaster a smile and move forward with you.
Forget that one night that remains in view.
I was always yours, even lying in his arms.
No need to disrupt what we've built, no cause to alarm.
Telling on myself would only free me from my remorse and shame
While your receiving ear would never look at me the same.
I swat away thoughts of being inadequate, I'm human after all.

I am still yours, in that I proudly stand tall.

Indiscretions

My intention was never to hurt you
It was to feed my emptiness,
I didn't stop to think of what you would go through
I just wanted to stop feeling so stressed.
So yea I admit I gave myself to someone else
Not worrying about the pain it would cause,
I found it liberating to once again be myself
And not persecuted for all my flaws.
So here I stand before you admitting my indiscretions
Hoping you find it in yourself to forgive.
I have come to learn the hard way from this lesson
A life without you is no way to live.
You've got to understand I felt suffocated
And you made me feel misunderstood.
So my payback for constantly getting berated
Was to be with someone who made me feel good.
I won't lie to you and tell you my emotions weren't caught in it
Please understand the grass was greener so I lost myself for a
minute.
I was so ready to walk away from all that we built
And turn a hardened heart toward you.
I never imagined I would feel this amount of guilt
Begging for your love and a chance of a redo.
No, don't turn your back on us
We can mend this relationship.
I'll work tirelessly to gain your trust

I'll even begin at friendship.
I get it, I crossed an unforgivable line
Where I've got you feeling insecure,
Constant images that haunt your mind
Leaves you unable to be how you were before.
I can see the pain in your eyes
And feel the ache in your heartbeat,
Your logic tells you to kiss us goodbye
For it makes no sense to be with a cheat.
Because even if you could move on and find it within to be with me
A part of you will never be able to escape the fact I gave another a
piece of me.

Grasping

I shed tears of aggravation
My heart remains in obliteration
From broken promises off your lying lips.
My heart's in so many pieces
Shattered in unfixable pieces
I can no longer go on like this.
The man that once warmed me so
Now has me feeling so cold
With nothing to look forward to.
The pain is my companion now
Happiness I can't allow
That reality is not my truth.
For the moment I let you in
I felt that you were the end
To a beginning of happily ever after.
The harsh realization
From the constant deprivation
Showed me I would never matter.
I am left starved and cut off
Stripped away of sight I am lost
Who am I without you?
Empty, a shallow form
Visibly, completely torn
You tell me what am I to do?
Try and erase you from my mind?
To forget your heartbeat matches mine?
The idea is impossible.

Disregard your paralyzing effect on me?
Ignore your effortless hold on me?
Now you know that's unfathomable.
Memories of you so vivid
I can't will myself to be livid
It's you that's my soulmate.
I'll clutch onto our past
Praying the memories will last
Until your love outweighs your hate.

kNOw Peace

Despondence
Depression
Despair
All of which I feel when I m with you.
Hope
Faith
Trust
All shattered because of you.
Sacrifices
Turning down opportunities
Just to remain by your s de.
Ungratefulness
No appreciation
I'm slowly dying inside.
Hate
Indifference
Separation
All of which I mostly identify.
Lost
Confusion
Anger
It might be time to say good bye.
I've given my all
Which wasn't enough
Go on and give the call.
Time of death on expired love.
See I don't want to try no more

I see no reason to hold on
Don't blame me, you shut the door
Mentally you've been gone.
Foolish me in trying to fix
What was broken
When all you wanted was out.
The longer I stayed with you
Left my heart in the open
You still told me peace out.
Love is only a healing
When it's reciprocated
I finally get that now.
The more I held onto you
The more it was me you hated
I hope you find that peace now.

Baby's Daddy

My baby's daddy oops I mean father of my child
Can't you see that she needs you
To raise her in this wild.
Worldly pleasures I try to keep her from
I am not enough, she needs encouragement from someone
Else who will teach her to understand
The thoughts and intents of a good man.
She needs more than a bank only supplying financial help
She needs to know real love from a man and how strong it is felt.
I can describe to her what she shouldn't be attracted to
But she'll still go on chasing after every man trying to replace the
missing love of you.
I can take her on dates and buy her flowers, tell her how valuable
she is
However she'll only focus on the very man who ceases to exist.
She'll question every positive thing I tell her
She'll develop feelings of inadequacy and be insecure.
The love she yearns for will be what motivates her to settle down
with any guy off the street.
As long as she's got someone there to accept her, she won't give a
damn should he be a deadbeat.
She'll be his crutch, holding tight onto him not believing she deserves
any better.
She'll cut everyone out her life who tells her they shouldn't be
together.
She'll put her life on pause only to focus on him and build his dreams

46

Stay with him through the other women, despite her falling apart at the seams.

She'll get pregnant in attempts to change him and keep him in her life

Only to restart the same cycle for her own, he still won't make her his wife.

She'll be left feeling more broken than before, rejection stinging worse than when you turned your back and denied her your love

She'll be stuck in a miserable mindset that all men are the same, the anger won't allow her to evolve

So baby's daddy oops I mean father of my child

Will you please consider staying a while?

Not for me but for the blessing we have created

To teach her strong sense of self, her outlook will never be jaded.

She will be confident and know of her worth

Because daddy stuck around and kept her first.

Jury

I plead guilty for making empty promises that led you to believe we had a future.
I plead guilty to not consistently being there for you and our child and leaving you on the back burner.
I didn't know how to balance your needs and ensure mine were met
So instead of trying a little harder, you had to pay the cost while I left.
I plead guilty to your emotional state for I am to blame for your bitter disposition.
I didn't safeguard your heart as I promised I would, I simply ignored your position.
I saw you as an inconvenience and I hated to fight over what was mine
I refused to hear you out and let you get what you needed to say off your mind.
I pushed you away mother of my child
Just so I could figure myself out for a while.
In the process of doing me, you were losing you.
Losing sleep on a child I should've been there for.
Losing sleep over the broken heart I caused.
I plead guilty for never taking the time to apologize and let you get that closure.
I plead guilty for all the suffering you endured in silence because you couldn't call on me.
I stand before you today, asking for a second chance.

To be the father I should've always been and be the support you need.
Forgive me for leaving you behind to focus on my future
Expecting your life to be on pause until I was ready to reconvene.
I'm not that man anymore I understand my transgressions
Moving forward I promise to be the father our child deserves for she's our greatest blessing.

Karma

If I can just find it in me to break out this vicious cycle
Put my hand on the bible and breathe.
Accept.
Forget.
Forgive.
Live.
If I could just expel all the negative emotions
This never ending hurt that keeps floating
On the inside.
Rejection.
Mistake.
Stupid.
Pitiful.
Instead I find myself in the pitfalls
Of constant ridicule
Incessant questioning of why I do what I do.
Like a cocoon, I wrap myself in the very thing that causes me to
destruct.
Believing that whomever I come into contact with I am their bad luck.
I am their end.
Dressed as a frienc
I see them as they are, the enemy.
Targeting them where it hurts before they have a chance to hit me.
I never tire of the betrayal plastered on their faces
The look of their disgraces

Because I won.

In my triumph I have no one to celebrate with

Since I've pushed everyone past their limit

I'm all alone.

The thought while a fleeting one, makes me cringe for a while

Before I'm reminded living in this wild

It's eat or get eaten

Defend or get beaten.

See my scars from the past.

They are all why I'm on attack.

I refuse to let anyone in

Like a lion, this is my den.

Try to understand my position

How man after man, only sought acquisition.

Just when I placed them on that pedestal, they'd disappear.

Imagine the pain I endured once I learned he's settled over there

With another.

So it wasn't them it was me

And the heart I gave so easily.

So like a tornado I destroy anyone in my path.

Not one to let go until they feel my wrath.

Now you go be broken

And attempt to heal

Deal with the string of emotions

That I've left you to feel.

No there's no remorse, not a regretful bone in my body

Understand that once you hurt the victim so much, she will turn on everybody.

Unconditional Love

Where I was broken in pieces, He made me whole
Led me to my purpose.
He said, "whenever you are ready to, know that you can trust me
with your soul."
And forever I would be His.
There is no turning His back on me, leaving me a mess
And expecting me to find my own way.
However I should understand there will be tests
And to conquer them, I must always pray.
"Some days I will need you to be a testimony for the non-believer
It's imperative you remain strong"
He equips me with the essentials therefore I'm an achiever
With His love I can do no wrong.
See I'm made to be a service to Him in any way that I can
It is He who restores and replenishes so that I carry out His plan.
It is not my place to question His authority
Or the road He tells me to go
Trusting that He only wants what's best for me
Ensures that I will certainly grow.
Long ago, I thought I was in control of my fate
Answered to no one but myself
I found I was consumed in fear and hate
He waited with open arms to help.
"My child, you are worth so much more than this
Allow me to be your peace,
"All that is required is your unwavering worship

And your troubles will decrease."
This life isn't meant to be easy, His strength will carry me through
Accept Him as your personal savior and see what He will do.

Hope

She never gives into the notion
That all men are broken
And possess the inability to love.
She knows finding the right woman
Will force the good man within to be summoned
So she's never quick to judge.
She's been known to give plenty a chance
Unbiased in choosing a certain man
She quickly gets involved.
While she lets him do the courting
She falls into the role of supporting
She believes there's nothing they can't solve.
The more time elapses
The more her life collapses
To fit into a world of their own.
Like the others before him
He abruptly puts an end
To the construction of their home.
Just like the many times before
She's hurt to the core
Her tears serve as a comforter.
Getting herself together as best as she can
She's still open to finding a good man
He's still out there, waiting for her.

The Other Woman part 2

It all began to make sense to me
She was the the lady
That kept you here with me.
It's like you stayed by default
Couldn't accept my faults
I felt under attack, assault.
Was loving me so impossible
Because I was incorrigible
Or did the good just feel miserable?
She was an extension of me
The best parts of me
Which made you love her unconditionally.
She didn't know the harshness of this world
How cruel society could be to a girl.
Her innocence remained furled
Neatly packaged in the compartments of her heart
Her mind only saw the good parts
She was not jaded by cruelty that people would impart.
I bear the brunt of the evil happenings
So I did not possess the trait of laughing
Through pain, my spirit was consumed in crackling.
Rapid succession of broken pieces between my heart and mind
How could I offer you better parts of me, where I was still trying to find
The balance between you and the world, left me in a bind.
What I gave you should've drawn you closer to me

Instead it pushed you further into her arms see,
I just was filler to your cavity.
Temporarily offering relief but pain was my modus operandi
I was too broken from life's troubles to ever let you in to understand me.
I wanted you to fight, to still love me past my hard exterior
I needed you to understand she was who I was in my interior
My intention was never to make you feel inferior
How could I show you otherwise, when I don't know what it is to be superior?
So I'm left to accept
She's your reason you don't step
She's the relief in your deep breaths
While I'm the one who makes you feel like death.
How do I even begin to correct
When she's all I have left
Of the person I seemed to forget?

Tantalize

You ever know someone that speaks to you? Now hear me when I
say this.
He speaks to the parts of you, you don't even say out loud.
He commands your attention, stands out effortlessly in a crowd.
Just at the sight of his name on your screen, you want to scream like
a boy crazed teen.
Break out into a fit of giggles not sure why you're suddenly so happy.
I mean the moment you hear the timbre in his voice you get weak.
You're unable to coherently form sentences to speak.
Then there's when you see him face to face
You instantly get the shakes.
Trembling as if your body is immersed in ice
Only to realize it's the heat that's got you burning inside.
He pulls you on this ride with him
And even though you know he'll leave in the end
You follow blindly. Willingly.
Hoping. Praying.
This time will be different.

Reminisce

Remember the time we would abandon responsibilities just to stay laid up in each other's arms?
The moments you would be ready to take on whomever and whatever might cause me harm?
The days you felt inspired just to buy me flowers to show me I'm in your thoughts.
The nights you held me closer to you even if we just fought.
The dates you took me on on a random Wednesday just to give me rest.
The times I came home to find you waiting for me and let me lay on your chest.
As time progresses we left the things that made us we.
I find that now that you feel secure, you see no reason to court me.
Trapped in a life of monotony, I feel suffocated, who do I turn to?
Although I know you're still that man beneath the cover up, I don't recognize you.
When we dated, you treated me as the latest hot commodity
Year after year it seems as if I have diminished in my quality
And you no longer feel the need to impress.
I try to ignore the mounting stress
And reason everything will go back to how we were before.
Denial is an easier pill to swallow than to accept the closed romantic door.
I still love you as I always have and cherish you as I always will
Praying incessantly you return to the man that excited me effortlessly and always fulfilled.

Acceptance

I have learned to cope without you
To accept a life without you.
I hold on to the memories of what we used to have.
Sadly understanding there is no turning back.
The shadow of who you used to be haunts me
The figure of who you are now doesn't have room for me.
You once called me soulmate, your bestfriend, and lover.
It's hard seeing you and knowing you're with another.
Imagining the same hands that once caressed me now touches her
The same lips that pressed against me now praises her.
I was your Eve!
Maybe that was the problem.
Instead of adding to your strengths, you saw me as your weakness.
Forbidden fruit has always had an expiration.
And while you have moved on so effortlessly, it is I who remains
stuck in a daze of who we used to be.
It is I who remains transfixed by your absence and this unrelenting
reality.
Day after day it's a deafening reminder you're not here.
Night after night, the emptiness that accompanies me is too much to
bear.
I take solace in what we once had
And I will learn to accept you are meant to stay in my past.

Foolish

I can tell you I'm tired of your constant vacillation between loving me and hating me.
One day you're sweet on me and the next, I'm the equivalent of a stranger to you.
My heart is quite like a pendulum swinging from one extreme to the next.
This roller coaster of emotions has me sick yet I'm still by your side.
Foolishly waiting for the next adrenaline rush, a feeling of euphoria.
Just to quickly come down from my high from the coldness of your shoulder.
I am so tired of questioning why and making excuses for your erratic behavior.
I'm more tired of when you do come back, the weakness I feel and how easily I fall back into you.
Sometimes I want the escape and feel like I deserve better.
Other times I feel after you, there is no one better.
I collect the pieces of me that you so callously toss away
And repair myself just to be broken again
All because,
With you,
It's always worth it.

My Piece

Excuse me as I may be a little bitter while I contemplate my way
through this dilemma.
You sought after me day after day, filling me in on your day to day.
Expressing your unhappiness with her, your discontent with her lack
of content.
How easy you portrayed it to be with me, how willingly I fell into your
deception effortlessly.
Though you've hurt me many times before, I forgive you and move
on, still allowing you access through that door.
The door to my heart, the key you've always had in your possession.
When will I be fed up enough to walk away is something I question.
I am privy to what you share with her and still I stay.
Foolishly expecting you to come be with me one day.
The ache in my chest as I read your words of pleasantness.
Calling her your peace, your soul mate and one desire.
Where was this peace when just the other day I extinguished your
fire?
Was she your peace as you sat and vowed undying love to me?
Was she your peace as you laboriously licked on my lips begging me
to release?
Was she your peace as you sucked on my bosom as a newborn to
its mother?
Was she your peace even when you told me I was like no other?
Where was this peace as you poured out your heart of how trapped
you feel?
Where was this peace as you wished that you and I could be
together for real?

I am baffled by your betrayal and shocked by my naïveté.

But more so I'm in a world of hurt from the love for her you display.

I'm wounded in the shadows waiting stupidly for you to come back to me.

The realization is too much to grasp that you are done since you've gotten your piece of me.

Lost

I am so utterly confused by your actions.
One day we're thick as thieves and the next we're estranged as strangers.
Stupid me, I allow you back in
When all I want to do is walk away.
My heart can't seem to make the connection you're bad for me.
My mind stays focused on the man I wish you to be.
I'm left hurting, feeling an inoperable pain
Only you could alleviate.
The times you are disguised as my knight
I willingly forget all the painful nights.
The nights I would cry trying to understand your bipolar disposition toward me.
The nights I had to soothe myself because you have decided to once again leave.
I. Am. Human.
I love you and I place myself in these painful situations thinking you love me also.
When in reality, your obsession is to cause me pain just to see my open arms lie in waiting for you.
Unbeknownst to me, I've become your punching bag and not the peace you are to me.
So after you've used me up, you disappear leaving me to fix myself up just enough for you to tear me down again.
Enough is enough.
I'm not only fed up with you. I am fed up with me.
Loving you more than me places me in a battlefield with no armor.
So suit up my dear, there's a change coming.

Blind

On the outside it appeared I was winning
Inside I always felt II was losing because I was missing you.
Our bond was undeniable from the beginning.
Easy conversation and mind blowing chemistry that was through the
roof.
Anyone in our presence could feel our love
And that made it all the more special.
You gave me butterflies I was proud of
And your actions outweighed your potential.
The hardest part was the momentary glimpses
And the fact you belonged elsewhere.
Because as soon as we said goodbyes you were someone different
Standing by her side, I knew you would never go anywhere.
I mindlessly accepted each blow
Each pang in my chest
Because you're the greatest love I ever will know
It is you that beats out the rest.
So I plaster my smile for the world to see
When inside I'm hurting miserably.
Despite the disarray going on within
I refuse to let them see me phased, so I continue to win.

Sadness

The first time it was like a stab in my heart
Having to receive your words of departure.
I existed, days after not really feeling much of anything.
The hardest part was to keep myself from reaching out to you
For deep down I knew.
Months went by and though I still felt pain, it was suddenly bearable.
I didn't cry as much
In fact I smiled more,
Accepting that on some level you were out there feeling the same joy
you gave to me.
Like an unsuspecting tornado, you were back in my life.
Naturally, we picked back up where we left off.
Never missing a beat.
The beat of my heart returned to its natural vibrancy.
The glow I had was indicative that you were now back to me.
I couldn't explain the hold you had over me and
How willing I was to put everything on hold for you.
I just knew.

This time around, no explanation has been given.
I'm shunned by your silence and this pain supersedes the first time.
I replay all our moments up until the silence.
Grasping and trying to explain your absence.   I have none.
I must accept that I'm just not enough for you.
Where you are my everything, I'm nothing to you.
No greater pain exists more than knowing at the end of the day,
This is all we'll ever be.

You

I used to think love was synonymous with pain
An unrelenting hurt that kept you in its grasp
Even when you swore you wouldn't return again.
I used to think the hurt was necessary for it to be real
So the countless lies you told, the numerous women you bedded
It was only the norm for me to eventually forgive and heal.
It wasn't until I took a look in the mirror
That I began to see clearer.
The pain and you were synonymous
And you were the high I kept chasing.
Like a needle in my vein, your love felt good
Until it was time to deal with the pain.
Unrequited actions of love
You behaved as if I were delusional.
All the years I spent trapped in your world
When all along I had the key
To set myself free.
See I didn't get that the temporary high I experienced was just that.
Temporary.
Because once that moment was over,
You passed me over like a beggar on the street.
You talked down to me like an enemy
And continued to chase these other women on the streets.
My pain lasted longer than the high you ever gave me
And it didn't hit home until I learned to love me.
To cherish my worth and what all I had to offer
To understand that your love caused more harm than good.
And that wasn't love.
I thank you for the pain and experience you gave

But more than ever, I'm grateful I now know love doesn't kill, it saves.
Fly

When you're on that ledge
Two things can happen:
You'll plummet to your death
Or you'll fly.
There are things in this universe
That are yours for the taking
Take a deep breath
See past what meets the eye.
Don't give in to the naysayers
Trying to blanket you with their negativity
Or fear of flying.
In order to achieve anything you've got to be a player
Filled with positivity
No use in not trying.
For when we do, each step forward
Is a mark toward success
Which moves us toward
Being ahead of the rest.
Those who remain on the ledge:
Scared.
Incapable.
Immobilized by what's ahead.
Your vision must supersede the potential obstacles
Your motivation outweigh the reasons why it can't be done.
Because when you've made it, you'll be that spectacle
And all it took was one.
One moment to forget the potential disappointments,
One action to spread your arms in preparation to soar,
One undying will to stay in constant movement,

One step that will open many a door.
The answers may not be 'yes' right away
Yet "not right now" is closer than a no.
And in order for you to meet success one day
"Not right now" is essential for growth.
Embrace the hardship
Tackle the difficulties
For any long standing relationship
Struggle is a necessity.
So stand on the ledge
Proud and strong
Let your vision be greater than what you see ahead
And you find where you've always belonged.